To Alan, a kindred spirit

MUSIC FOR LIVING

bimh Publications

MUSIC FOR LIVING

enriching the lives of profoundly mentally handicapped people

Miriam Wood

Illustrations: David Baird

Photographs: James D. Gilford

First published 1982

(Registered Charity 264786),
Wolverhampton Road,
Kidderminster, Worcs. DY10 3PP

ISBN 0 906054 47 8

Printed by
CIP Ltd., Brierley Hill, West Midlands

Contents

Foreword

Music has enriched the lives of millions, speaking often where words have failed. Miriam Wood, in writing this booklet, has committed to paper many of her personal experiences while working with mentally handicapped people at a small hospital in East Berkshire. In demonstrating enthusiasm and using a natural ability, she has been able to encourage those around her to share experiences.

Keeping a balance of opportunities is fundamental to any training programme for the mentally handicapped, but what is more important is never to ignore natural talents and natural abilities, whether these are found in teachers or pupils.

Miriam Wood has written in terms that everyone involved in caring for mentally handicapped people can understand. Her booklet will certainly provide guidance and encouragement for others.

COLIN J. HARRIS
Administrator,
Health Services for the Mentally Handicapped in East Berkshire

Acknowledgements

Thanks are expressed: to the staff of Church Hill House Hospital, Bracknell, who daily make possible music and other training programmes for the residents; to Berkshire Area Health Authority for support prior to reorganisation; to Alan Norvil, who laid the foundations for music within the hospital; to Jim, who gave up a week's holiday to photograph the residents; to Mr. W. T. Henning, Senior Nursing Officer, Church Hill House Hospital and Mr. C. J. Harris, Sector Administrator (East Berkshire), for their helpful advice and suggestions; to Miss D. Kennard, Music Adviser, Disabled Living Foundation, for her help and encouragement over the years and aid in compiling the addresses and book list; and to the British Institute of Mental Handicap for publishing the booklet.

Miriam Wood

Introduction

Music brings enjoyment to the majority of people, handicapped or not, but planning the best way to use music for the benefit and development of the profoundly mentally handicapped presents many problems as well as rewards.

By the term "profoundly handicapped" I am referring to the least able persons in the severely mentally handicapped category. This includes : those who are physically and mentally handicapped, and who show little or no response to their surroundings; those who are able to walk, but whose mental ability is extremely limited; those who can walk, but who have other physical handicaps such as deafness or blindness and a low mental ability; and those who have a low mental ability plus additional difficulties such as autism or a severe behaviour problem.

Profoundly handicapped people may show signs of pleasure whilst listening to music — by laughing, "singing", clapping, or rocking — but how can those involved in caring use these reactions to music to encourage development ?

We need a basic starting point in order that the least able persons can be involved, yet the programme must be arranged so that development can take place and so that those with latent ability need not be deprived of expressing themselves.

This booklet describes methods and exercises developed through practical experience. Activities that normal young children can join in enthusiastically are too complex for most profoundly mentally handicapped people. For example, simple concepts, such as holding hands or sitting down on cue as in the classic *Ring o' Roses*, have to be taught.

By using music we have an immediate advantage — it is a language which speaks where words are not understood. An increasing number of those who care for mentally handicapped people are finding carefully constructed music programmes of great benefit. Britain has been slow to recognise the therapeutic use of music with the profoundly handicapped. Practical experience has shown that music does help in a variety of ways, not only by providing pleasure — although this is equally important for individuals whose ability to enjoy life is very poor. Music can be used as a means of reaching the autistic, bringing achievable goals into the lives of people with severe physical handicaps, forming the basis of a training programme, and encouraging speech where little or none exists.

The British Society for Music Therapy, founded in 1958, has done much to bring the use of music to the fore. Miss Juliette Alvin, the founder, has written many books on the subject. Music therapists are trained at the Guildhall School of Music (Miss Alvin), at Roehampton Institute of Higher Education (Miss Elaine Streeter), or at the Nordoff-Robbins Music Therapy Centre, in cooperation with The City University (Miss S. Beresford Peirse). Other music teachers have specialised in the use of music with the handicapped and published books on the subject (for example Phillip Bailey, 1973; David Ward, 1975). Each has given examples of people with whom they have worked and of the benefit that music brings.

In preparing structured programmes for the most severely handicapped people, the problem is one of simplicity. It is surprisingly difficult to reduce activities to their simplest form in order to find a starting point and a plan for development. Some individuals will be able to begin at an intermediate point, or will progress rapidly from the simplest point. Others may take a long time to grasp the first step. It is necessary to find the point of response for each person. Those working with the handicapped need to become aware of this response, note it, and then build on it.

This booklet is written from experience of working with young people whose mental ability is severely limited, the majority of whom have one or more additional handicap (such as hearing loss, blindness, the appearance of autistic features, or a physical handicap). Time and experience have proved that it is possible to include the majority in training which has a strong musical element.

The place of music

Music can be used to stimulate and help in a variety of situations. Here are some suggestions.

In the home

Parents of a handicapped child or adult may find that music can be a bridge between the handicapped person and other members of the family. A choice of records for listening can interest all members of the family and build up relationships. Action songs and the use of live music can help development. Children growing up in the household can be encouraged to learn music and play to a handicapped brother or sister, perhaps teaching them to sing a little, or join in with percussion instruments. Relaxing music as part of a bed-time "ritual" can have a soothing effect and promote sound sleep. Likewise, music played at certain times of the day can become a signal of an event about to happen.

Hospital wards

The most obvious value of music in a hospital ward is entertainment. However, many handicapped people are subjected to non-stop music of mainly one type ("pop" music) from morning until night. Care should be taken in the choice and variety of music played and quiet times should be provided. It is erroneous to think that mentally handicapped people cannot enjoy listening to classical music. Even the most handicapped show a preference for certain types of music.

Too often the radio, television, and record player are in conflict with one another, causing confusion rather than a happy atmosphere. Music making, music and movement, and song sessions can be used with benefit, and specific times should be set aside each day for these activities to take place. The sessions need not take long (maybe half-an-hour is sufficient), but regularity can make them an event which is anticipated. They provide interest for both staff and residents.

Special care units

A unit designed to care for the profoundly mentally handicapped should provide a room, or section of a room, where staff interested in the use of music can take individuals or groups and provide musical activities. Exercises to music for the physically handicapped may be very useful, but a variety of activities can take place according to ability. It is easy to underestimate the potential. Sometimes, learning to participate in an active way may take months or years. Once the "key" has been found and a door unlocked, then the unexpected may happen.

Recreation department

In some hospitals the recreation staff provide music programmes for the residents. Usually a hall with a piano is available. This is ideal for movement and music, and for music concerts specially designed for the residents (see address *Council for Music in Hospitals*). Drama can be linked with music as this department will be expected to provide programmes for groups of residents whose abilities are varied.

Training programme — basis for

When a training programme is being set up, either on an individual or group basis, it is often difficult to know where to begin, especially when it is expected that response will be limited. Music, because it has immediate impact, can be used to advantage. Sessions may include music and movement for those able to walk, individual and group music making, physiotherapy exercises to music, and songs to stimulate speech or to teach sign language. All of these can be used to develop whatever spark of ability is obvious from the beginning or emerges in the course of a programme.

Setting up a music programme

As with any project there is the ideal situation (special room, plenty of instruments, a trained music therapist, and plenty of helpers), a workable basic (a dual purpose area, one or two instruments, one member of staff interested in using music but having only a little ability), and a less than suitable situation (no regular room available, no instruments, and no-one who claims to have any musical knowledge). Many music programmes would never begin if the ideal conditions were awaited. However, if a start is made with whatever is available, help and equipment can be gathered as time goes on. Voluntary organisations are often willing to help with equipment when a programme is already established.

Staff

The most important part of any music programme is the leader. The programme's success or failure depends on that person having interest and vision. If two people can co-operate with each other, there are even more advantages. Other helpers will then be encouraged to assist in sessions that require additional help, such as movement and music activities.

Need the person in charge of music be a qualified musician? Preferably yes. An interested person with qualifications is probably the right one to choose, but it is equally important that the person chosen can relate well to the residents and use his or her own musical ability for their benefit. Staff who feel the benefit that music brings to the mentally handicapped, but who have a limited practical musical ability, can develop a useful programme with guidance.

If no-one in the training team is musically inclined, volunteers (local music teachers, music students, groups from local schools) may be able to help. Otherwise, amongst the staff there may be someone with a love of music prepared to begin by using songs, learning a few chords on the guitar, playing a melody and bass chords on a piano or a chord organ, or using carefully chosen recorded music either for listening to or to accompany various exercises. Once involved, encourage the staff member to develop musical skills through courses which will help that person's ability to train the mentally handicapped using music.

The attitude of the staff members and their ability to relate to people with very severe handicaps is as important as the music.

Equipment

It is wise to buy good, strong equipment which has a pleasing tone. Initially it may be necessary to borrow or make equipment but the aim should be to purchase equipment of good quality. If the instruments are used carefully in an organised programme (not scattered at random for the residents to treat roughly) they will last much longer. When a programme is established and its usefulness proven, it is easier to obtain money for instruments. Charities may also be prepared to help.

Accommodation

For group or individual music making, choose a room where there are few distractions (for example, not a room leading into another area, or where passers-by or noise distracts). If a small room is not available, screen off an area of a larger room or hall, and try to limit distractions. Once a music session has begun there should be no interruptions until it ends. This is most important, as a response by a resident should be followed up at once. If distracted, the same response may not happen again for weeks, or it could be lost forever.

Length of programme

Regularity of programmes is more important than lengthy sessions. Half an hour spent with a group at a regular time (one to five times) each week is far more beneficial than an irregular hour or two only when time is available.

Number in groups

Music making sessions for groups of 4-8 handicapped people with two staff can be successful, depending on the kind of persons involved. If group members are overactive or present behaviour problems it may be necessary to have additional helpers (in the ratio of one-to-one or one-to-two) so that the programmes can progress. Careful selection of group members in order to make a balanced group (that is, not all the most difficult individuals in one group) is very necessary if help is limited. Once formed, groups should remain together, members being changed only after careful consideration, as the balance can be upset by changes.

Movement sessions can involve more people (perhaps up to 12) depending on group members' ability to walk without aid. Larger groups can be divided, all helpers available working with each group for 15 to 20 minutes.

Physiotherapy exercises to music need a one-to-one support. The size of these groups will be determined by the number of helpers available and the number of group members needing special exercises.

Misuse of music

The right music at the right time

As music appeals to mentally handicapped people there is a tendency to over-use it, or to use it without thought. Everyone likes peace and quiet now and again. For example, the once popular idea of playing "canned music" in supermarkets seems to be dying out, as people need quiet to consider what they are buying. On the other hand, soft, relaxing music in some dental surgeries can have a very good effect at a time of stress. Soft lights and sweet music can set the mood for a romantic evening meal. "Disco" music, with flashing lights, produces a completely different atmosphere. It is important to provide the right music at the right time, or silence when needed.

Think, then, when using music with people who have no choice but to listen to it as they are unable to switch it off or leave the area where it is played. Do not use constant "pop" music as it can have a disturbing effect over a long period. Have times of silence, and a variety of styles of music at various times of the day. Plan programmes carefully and make a serious use of music. Take things slowly.

When a resident begins to make progress in music, beware of putting too much pressure on him or her. For example, one young woman with no speech attended music sessions.

She clapped her hands to music and beat the tambourine, but would have no contact with a xylophone or key-board instrument. She seemed to enjoy being sung to, so songs were addressed to her and repetitive choruses sung slowly to emphasise the words. Suddenly one day she said, "Sit down," to one of the other residents. She began to look into the faces of staff, listen carefully to them, and to make sounds.

Because of this progress other staff began to show more interest in her and plan activities for her. She commenced a training programme to wash her hands and face which she did not particularly enjoy. On the ward where she lived, she began to help by moving chairs after meals. Then she began to demand more attention from staff in a quiet way. She also removed shoes from residents, took cardigans away, and emptied drawers in an attempt to find an outlet for her new-found awareness. Her attempts were not always relevant and caused problems. She became hyperactive both by day and by night and she began to sleep less and less. She found it difficult to swallow, so lost weight. Only careful medical attention, rest, and a special diet returned her to "normal". Now she is as she was before, within her own speechless world.

This taught us several lessons. Do not be over-enthusiastic when progress is made. Allow the person several months to consolidate any new skill without adding extra programmes. Communicate with the people caring for the person such as hospital or hostel staff, or parents if he or she lives at home and discuss the person's progress, make plans with their assistance, talk about any problems, and deal with them at once.

Music sessions in practice

When sessions are first organised they may need to be brief, perhaps of only 10 minutes' duration. Gradually lengthen the sessions as concentration and interest develop. It is important not to aim too high at first and so become discouraged when expectations are not reached.

The group leader's love of music and empathy with the residents is very important. He is not teaching music but is *using* it to reach people whose minds are not open to the world around them. Out of this experience learning may come, but for many handicapped people the atmosphere of the music sessions and a feeling of well-being may be their limit. This is equally rewarding for the leader and the group members, although it is very gratifying when strong evidence of development is seen.

Groups (preferably of not less than four and no more than eight) should be selected and kept together in the same session each time. In this way the group identity can be built up and group members become aware of each other. If changes are made for any reason it is best to replace one person at a time so that the group does not change drastically. It is important to have a balanced group. If one person is causing a nuisance, and does not settle after repeated efforts, it is probably better to remove him and try him in another group or alone.

It is good if the leader is able to make these decisions and is not forced to accept everyone who is "sent to music" in predetermined groups.

If sessions are disrupted by misbehaviour, incontinence, or other reasons, make the best of the situation, refuse to worry, and trust that the next session will be more profitable. It may be some while before sessions run smoothly and can be considered successful. Residents settle and progress better if their music programme is organised to take place daily as part of a wider training programme.

Use of instruments and voice in live music sessions

Music sessions for the profoundly mentally handicapped should be well planned, and careful consideration should be given to the choice of songs and instruments. The plan below may be a useful guide when deciding on the content of a music session.

PLAN OF MUSIC SESSION

Opening theme OR song

Name song OR greeting song

Educational rhythmics OR action songs

Live instrumental music for listening (introduce various instruments) OR recorded music of different musical styles (for example, folk, orchestral, organ, vocal, choral)

Sleigh bells or tambourines (for residents to accompany a song)

Development of residents' rhythm and pitch

Songs to encourage speech

Goodbye song.

Sit the residents around a table, or on chairs in a circle or semi-circle. It is best to begin each session in a definite way, using a signature tune or a song which can become familiar to the group. Continue with a variety of songs and the use of various instruments, giving each resident the opportunity to join in. Of necessity programmes will have a repetitive element. Profoundly mentally handicapped people love music that becomes familiar to them, and repetition is their only sure way of learning. However, music is so varied that it is possible to introduce variety into each session while maintaining a familiar structure.

EXERCISES

1. Use of drum to develop co-ordination, control, and rhythm

Make up words and sing them to a familiar tune, such as:

"Harry beat the drum,
Harry beat the drum,
Harry, Harry, Harry beat the drum".
(TUNE: The farmer's in his den)

Encourage resident to beat the drum and accompany him on an instrument (the piano is best). Alter rhythm and volume in order to lead him to respond. Be flexible and follow his beat too.

Encourage drum beat at the end of each line of a song, for example:

"If you're happy and you know it, beat the drum"
(beat-beat).

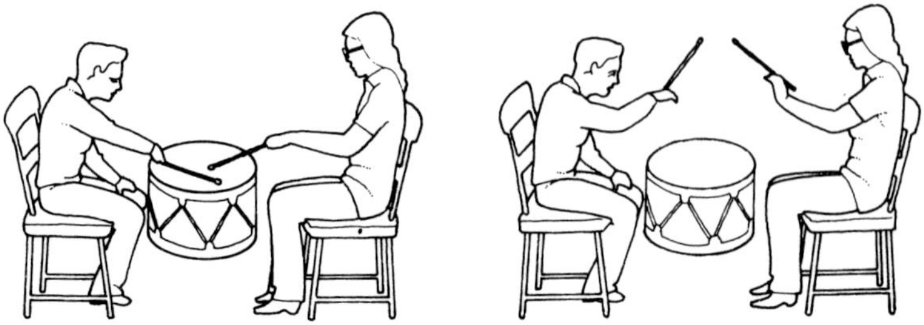

Leader and resident beat simultaneously on the drum, then raise arms (so missing a beat). They repeat this in a regular pattern, so encouraging an awareness of rhythm.

Leader and resident beat the drum in a conversational form to each other (that is, one after the other).

Sing and play songs to which residents can beat the drum following the rhythm of the words, for example:

x x x x x x x x
"Charlie knows how to beat that drum, ... "
Nordoff/Robbins, *The First Book of Children's Playsongs.*

2. Chime bars

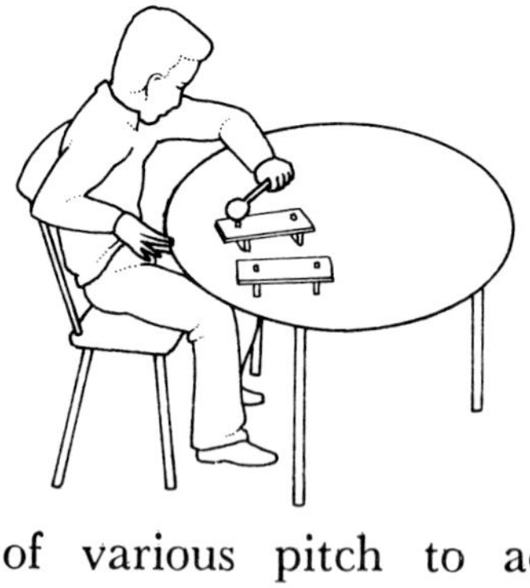

Use chime bars of various pitch to accompany songs. Encourage the resident to follow the rhythm of the words (as for the drum). At first it may be necessary to hold the resident's arm at the elbow to help him feel the rhythm and beat the chime bar.

"Hello"
Nordoff/Robbins, *Songs for children with resonator bells and piano.*

3. Songs to encourage pre-speech, speech, and eye contact

Sing to the group and to individuals. Use name songs and encourage residents to respond by making a sound, "singing", making eye-contact with leader, smiling, shaking hands, or singing words (Taskmaster, *Songs of Speech*). Use songs which encourage a reply, for example:

"Tony Jones . . where are you?"
"Here I am, here I am . . "

Imitate any vocal sounds that the resident makes, on an instrument, or by singing back to him. Initiate sounds for him to copy or to reply to.

4. Sleigh bells

Provide everyone with sleigh bells and make up a song about

shaking bells for them to accompany, such as:

"Shake the bells, shake the bells,
Shake, shake, shake the bells.
Sarah Williams shake the bells,
Shake, shake, shake the bells".

Add other verses, such as, "Everybody shake the bells" or "Shake the bells above your head" (. . . behind your back, and so on).

5. Dischords and harmony

Some residents who do not show response, or who respond to music in a repetitive manner such as rocking or swaying, are sometimes affected by the playing of dischords followed by harmony. Discordant music cuts across their withdrawn state. The harmony which follows is then more noticeable, and seems to give a feeling of security. They may smile, make eye-contact with helpers, or grasp an instrument.

6. Strumming a guitar

The sound of a guitar is attractive to many residents. When they reach out and touch it they feel the strings and body vibrate. Some residents strum the strings while the leader changes the chords and sings. It is very satisfying for them to be able to "play" an instrument in this way.

7. Touch-a-Tune organ

The notes on a normal piano or organ are too close together for profoundly mentally handicapped people to play one note at a time. The ***Touch-a-Tune organ*** (see addresses) has a flat keyboard, made up of large notes which can be played by the hand, arm, elbow, head, or feet. The sensitivity of the notes is variable and can be adjusted to suit individual needs. Each note is coloured. Make a colour code to teach simple melodies, or use the keyboard to help colour recognition. This instrument is very useful for the severely physically handicapped.

8. Music for listening

Music has so much variety; the range of instruments and styles is almost limitless. What may be attractive to one person may be less attractive to another person. The sound of a particular instrument may appeal more to one than to another, or a certain type of music may interest one person in particular.

Invite people who play an instrument to visit music sessions to play for a short while. (Young people learning instruments may be interested).*

Build up a varied selection of recorded music which includes excerpts from opera, folk music, orchestral music, organ, national music, strings, brass, and so on. These can bring an increased awareness of their environment to residents whose lives are egocentric, and can bring variety into very limited lives.

*The Council for Music in Hospitals arranges longer concerts to suit all needs.

9. *Action songs and educational rhythmics*

Small children love action songs. Likewise, mentally handicapped people of all ages enjoy learning and identifying parts of their body through music, or acting out songs. Educational rhythmics is a very enjoyable form of action to music (see BIMH publication, *Educational Rhythmics*).

Movement and music

Movement and music is very beneficial for profoundly mentally handicapped people whose movements are often unco-ordinated or without purpose. Planned movement to music can bring order out of chaos. It can help them to develop an awareness of others in the room, develop balance and co-ordination, encourage eye-contact, bring understanding of verbal commands, and produce co-operation and relaxation.

It is best not to involve too many residents initially. If possible have a helper/resident ratio of one-to-one or one-to-two. Residents who are not involved in sessions may be happy to sit and watch the activity. Begin with one or two simple exercises and gradually build up the programme to 15 or 20 minutes as the confidence of staff and residents increases.

EXERCISES

1. Circle

Hold hands in a circle and walk around a table (to give the circle shape). Walk to the left and then to the right.

Hold hands in a circle and walk to the left, then walk towards the centre and out again (backwards), several times. Walk to the right and then repeat movement to centre. Repeat several times and end by swinging arms (still holding hands) or swing legs.

MUSIC: Lively music with a refrain (example: *Dippety Day*, sung by Father Abraham).

2. Marching or musical bumps

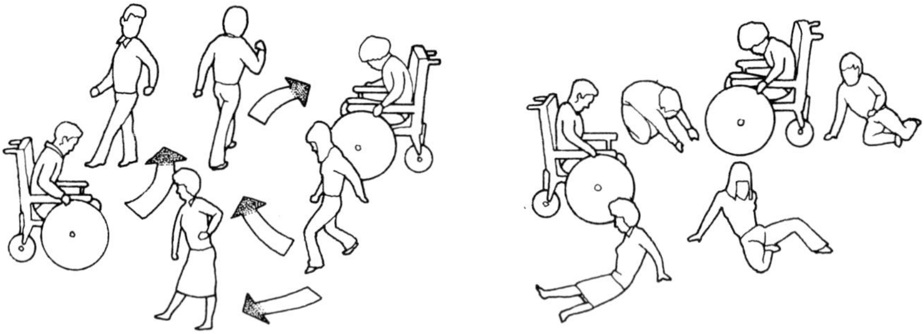

March around the room with residents who are able to walk, and around those in wheelchairs. Develop this exercise to become musical bumps, that is, sitting down when the music stops, and marching again when the music recommences.

MUSIC: Marching or other music with a strong beat at brisk

walking pace (examples: *Colonel Hathi's March* from the *Jungle Book* and *Colonel Bogey*).

3. *Two lines*

Form two lines, each made up of helpers and residents, who hold hands and face each other across the room. Line 1 walks across the room towards line 2, then retreats backwards. Line 2 repeats the action. Build in vocalisation on meeting. This develops balance, helps walking both backwards and forwards, and encourages eye contact and vocalisation.

MUSIC: Lively marching music (example: *The lonely goat-herd* from *The Sound of Music*).

4. *Passing an object*

Sit in a circle on the floor (or on chairs) and pass an object around the circle. Develop the exercise by passing two objects in opposite directions so that they meet and have to be passed on correctly. For contrast, use bells and a soft toy or pass a

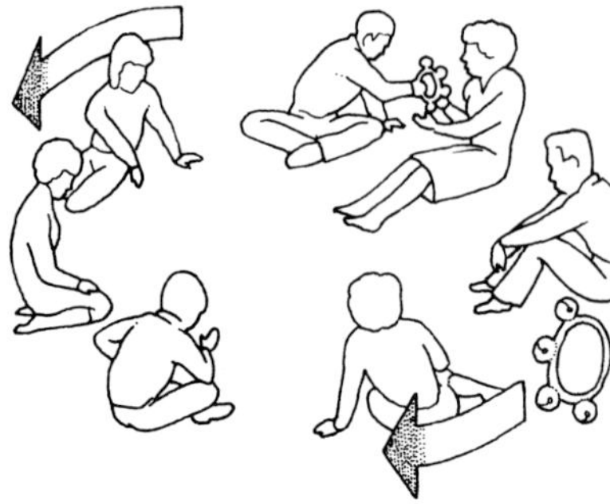

large and a small object. This exercise develops the sense of touch, aids concentration, and brings group awareness.

MUSIC: Quiet music with a gentle rhythm (example: *The Old Rocking Chair*).

5. Under and over objects

Use a table or tunnel, or build an arch of foam shapes. Place obstacles around the room (foam shapes or low benches). Walk around the room stepping over objects, walking under arches, or crawling under tables. This is useful for the development of awareness, balance and agility.

MUSIC: Lively rhythmic music but not too fast (example: *Paloma Blanca*).

6. *Trains*

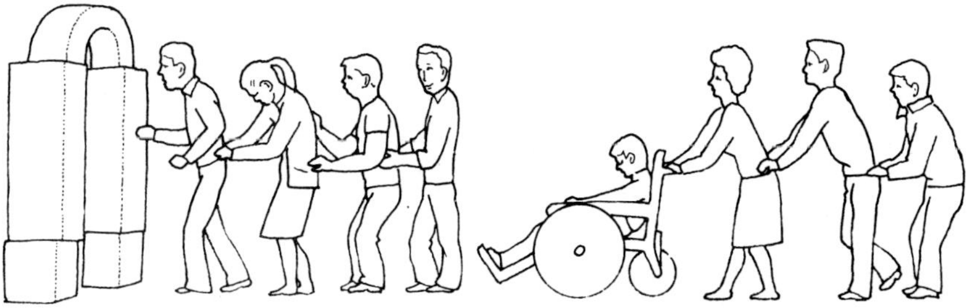

Hold the waist of the person in front and walk around the room and under an arch, or out of a door and up and down a corridor (if suitable). Wheelchairs can be pushed under the bridge and join in the "train".

MUSIC: Music which resembles or imitates the sound of a train OR a song about a train (examples: *The Runaway Train*; *Morning Town Ride*).

7. *Hoops*

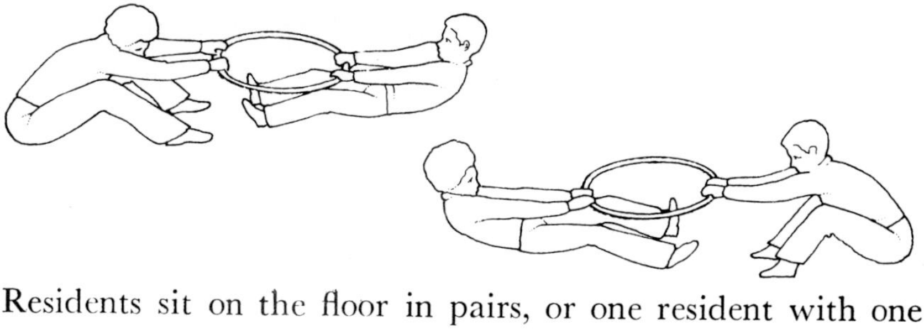

Residents sit on the floor in pairs, or one resident with one helper. Each pair holds a hoop and rocks backwards and forwards. The ultimate aim is complete co-operation, so that the resident lies back and is pulled up into a sitting position. This exercise builds up confidence, balance, co-operation and eye-contact.

MUSIC: Soft music with a gentle swinging feeling (example: *Kehar's Theme* from *Watership Down*).

8. Relaxation

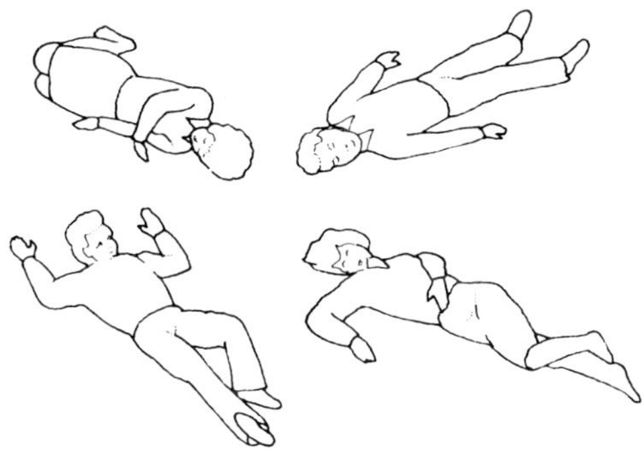

At the end of a group of exercises, lie on the floor on mats, rugs, or blankets. Encourage all residents and helpers to lie and listen to music for a few minutes. This aims to develop self control (lying quietly for a definite period) and relaxation.

MUSIC: Lullaby, a quiet song, or soothing orchestral music (example: *Serenade* by Drigo (James Galway on Flute); *Bright Eyes* by Art Garfunkel).

Movement for wheelchair residents (passive)

Handicapped people who are confined to wheelchairs are often excluded from activities which involve movement. However, most of those who can walk with help can be included in the previous exercises. For those who are unable to walk, even with support, the following exercises can be useful, the residents participating passively and the actions being initiated by the helper. Before any physically handicapped person commences these exercises, his physiotherapist should be consulted to ensure that they are suitable for him.

EXERCISES

1. Legs

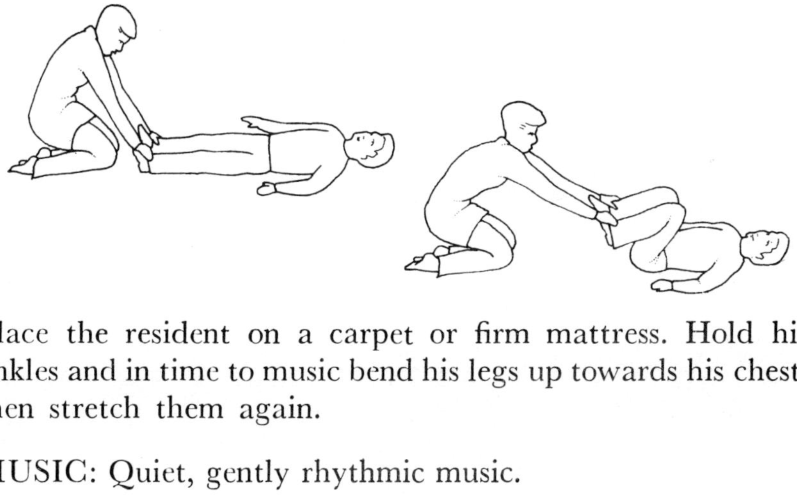

Place the resident on a carpet or firm mattress. Hold his ankles and in time to music bend his legs up towards his chest, then stretch them again.

MUSIC: Quiet, gently rhythmic music.

2. Hips

From the same starting position hold the ankles and gently

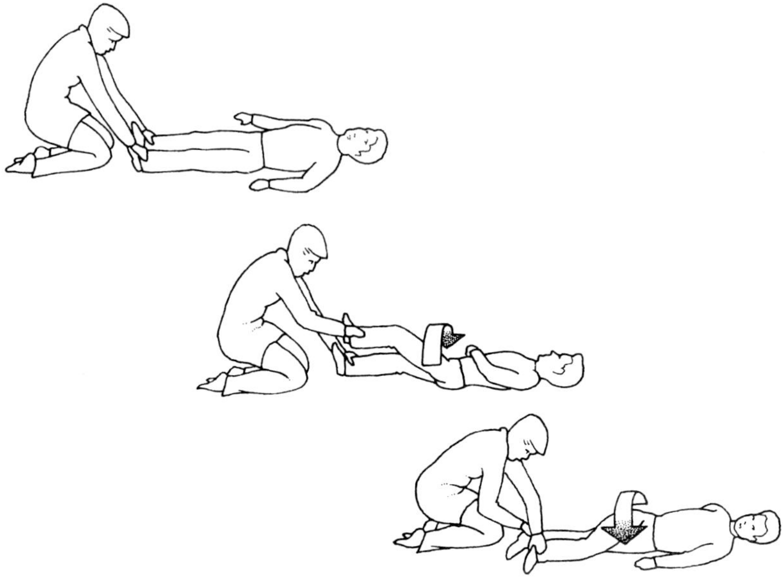

swing the person's legs from side to side, raising the left leg over the right and then the right leg over the left in order to exercise the hips:

MUSIC: Quiet waltz-time music.

3. Rolling

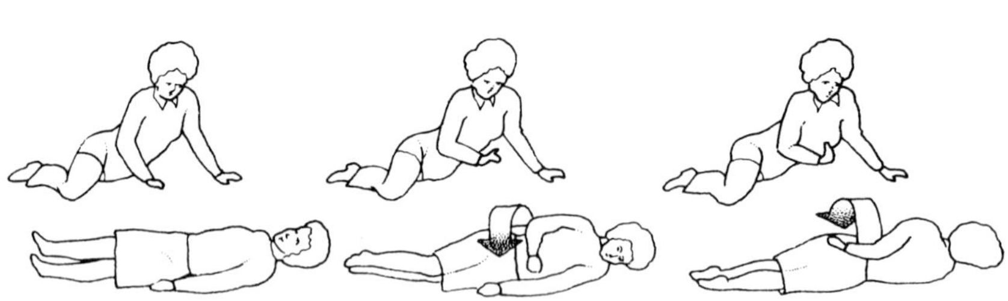

Begin with the resident on his back, then roll him on to one side and then on to the other. Give opportunity and encouragement for the resident to roll unaided.

MUSIC: A musical sound which depicts rolling, such as a drum roll or harp.

4. Arms

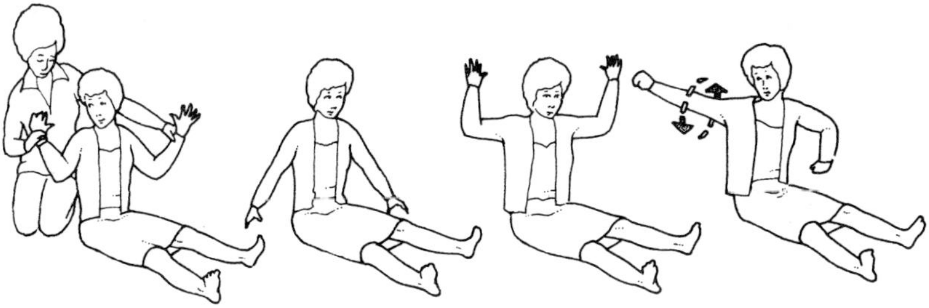

With the resident lying or sitting, gently bend and stretch his arms, or rotate them to exercise the shoulders. Concentrate the effort where there is least movement, but also exercise other parts to maintain flexibility.

MUSIC: Quiet rhythmic music of moderate speed.

5. Hands and wrists

Gently rotate wrists. Open and close hands, and bend and straighten fingers.

MUSIC: Music suggestive of circular movement on piano or harp.

6. Lying down and sitting up

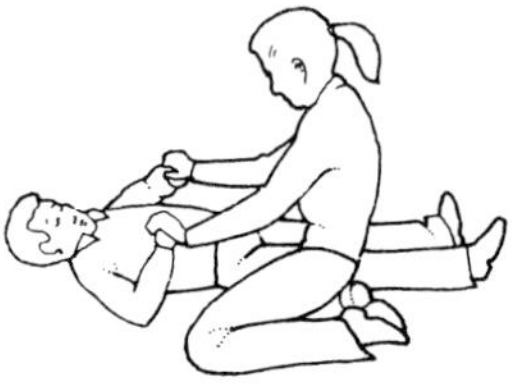

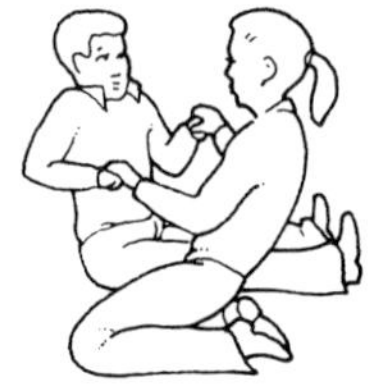

OR

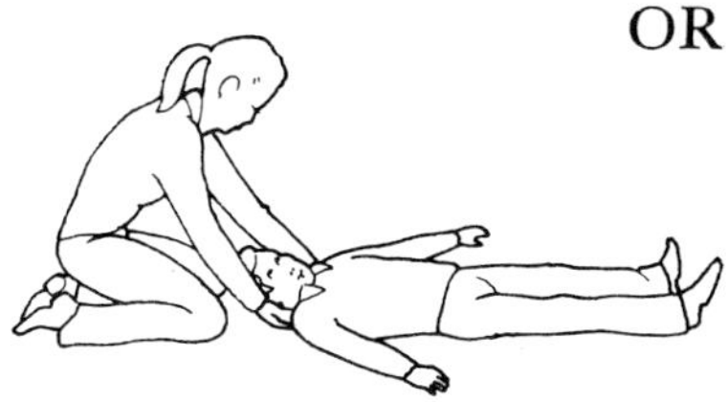

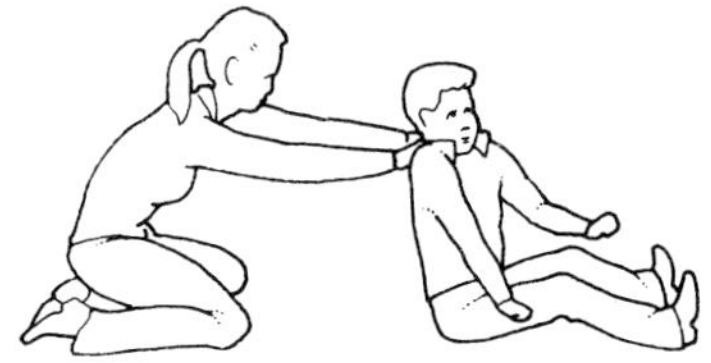

Begin with the resident lying down on his back. Raise him to a sitting position by holding his arms or hands while kneelng beside him, or by holding him at the shoulders while sitting behind him. Allow him to balance in a sitting position if possible, then lower him to the first position. Repeat the sequence until the end of the music.

MUSIC: Choose music which gives the feeling of raising and lowering and is not too fast.

7. Rocking

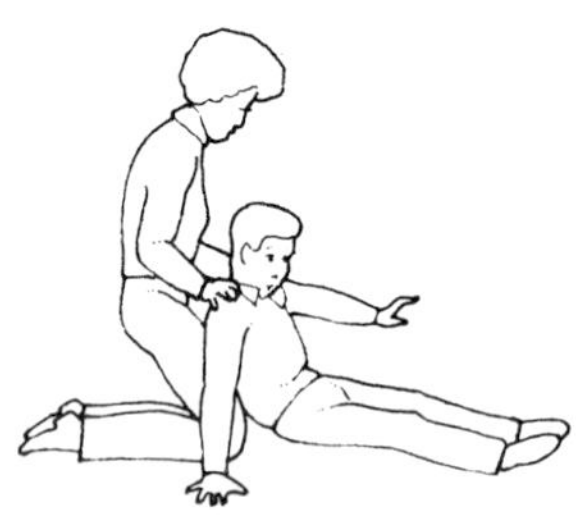

Sit behind the resident with your legs on either side of his body and gently rock him from side to side. If this position is not comfortable because the resident is too heavy, kneel behind him. Place his hands on the floor either side and encourage him to rock himself by pushing first on one hand and then the other.

MUSIC: Lullaby, or gentle rocking music.

Movement for wheelchair residents (active)

The following exercises are designed to encourage residents to participate actively without help. They can be carried out whilst seated in a wheelchair.

EXERCISES

1. Action songs

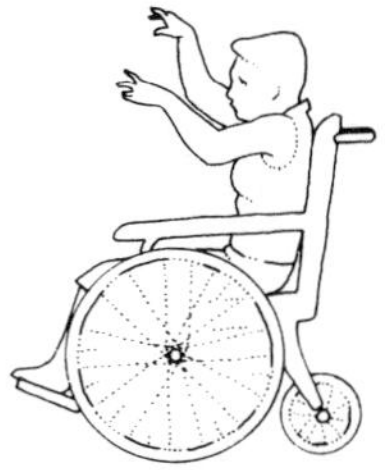

Make up songs to suit individual needs, such as, "Sandra, wave your arms". Sing and do the actions in order to encourage the resident to copy.

2. Swaying and bending

Consider the residents individually and what they are capable of doing. Encourage them to copy bending and swaying

OR

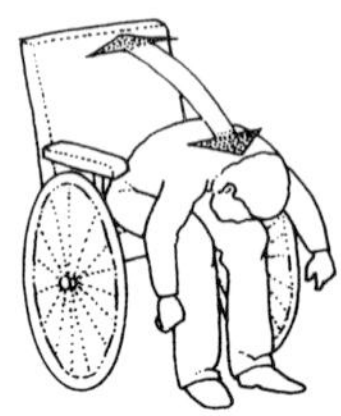

exercises, or hold them by the hands and physically encourage the movement if necessary.

3. Hoops

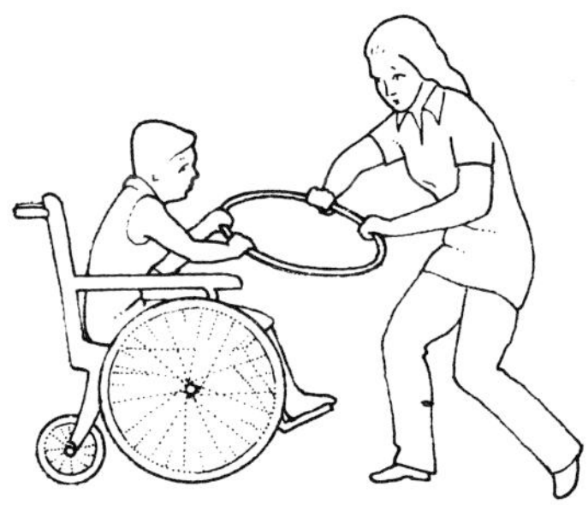

Hold a hoop with a resident and pull and push together with the brakes of his wheelchair released. Residents enjoy this, finding that by pulling and pushing on the hoop they can move their chairs backwards and forwards.

Assessment of progress

Progress is sometimes difficult to detect when it is slow, and when staff or parents are in daily contact with a handicapped person. It is, therefore, important to keep a record of each person's progress. If a group of residents attend music regularly it is very easy to work with the best in the group who are responding to activities, and to neglect the needs of those who are less responsive. By regular assessment the non-participants in the group can be included in the planning and can begin to progress.

Begin with an assessment of all the residents in a group after a few music sessions, when there has been time for each one to react to the various activities in his own way. Reassess at regular intervals, making sure that the date of each assessment is recorded. Also include a brief summing up of the individual's response to the sessions, and list his strengths and weaknesses and your aims for him. Set achievable goals for each person, for example eye contact during the singing of a name song; or development of concentration by use of a drum-beating exercise.

A questionnaire similar to the one given on the following two pages can be helpful.

INDIVIDUAL PROGRESS REPORT

Name :
Date of birth :
Sessions attended :

Date of assessment :
Completed by :

Live music session : graduated response

1. Does he
   a) show pleasure when music session begins?
   b) anticipate session by word, sign, excitement?
   c) find his own way into the room unaided, or make preparation by aiding leader with other residents, chairs, or musical equipment?

2. Does he
   a) look at person singing his name?
   b) recognise his own name and identify others when their names are sung?
   c) respond verbally to his name?

3. Will he
   a) shake hands with leader during a greeting song?
   b) shake hands with another resident?
   c) shake hands and join in with the song by humming tune or singing words?

4. Will he
   a) grasp sleigh bells, beater, or drum stick, and hold them for a short while?
   b) shake bells, or use beater or drum stick in an attempt to produce a sound on chime bars or drum?
   c) shake bells and stop when appropriate, beat rhythmically on chime bars or drum?

5. Does he
   a) attempt to hum when songs are sung?
   b) sing snatches of melody?
   c) sing complete melody, or join in with the words?

6. Does he
   a) show interest in listening to music?
   b) show preference for a particular style or piece of music?
   c) request by word or sign a particular piece of music?

Movement and music — general assessment

Does he join in the session willingly or reluctantly?

Will he hold hands with helpers and other residents when required?

Is he aware of when the music starts and stops?

Does he follow the pace of the music?

Is his balance improving? Can he walk backwards?

Does he notice where to sit to form a circle with other residents?

Does he watch objects as they are passed around, receive them, and pass them on?

Does he step over objects, and will he go under objects of various heights?

Will he (a) hold a hoop, (b) put effort into exercises using hoops?

Is his sociability improving?

Will he lie down for the duration of the relaxation exercise with/without help?

Movement for wheelchair residents — general assessment

Is he happy when placed on the floor to begin exercises? Describe reaction.

Is the movement of his limbs improving? List problems and improvements.

Is he becoming active during exercises rather than continuing to play a passive role? Specify his capability.

Summary of general response and progress

Personal encounters with music

The following people attend music sessions several times a week in groups of between 6 and 10. One member of staff can work alone with the smaller groups, though two do so when available and with the larger groups. Sessions take place in a room set aside for music in a training unit attached to the hospital where the profoundly mentally handicapped young people live. The unit also provides individual training programmes, "free expression" (sand and water play), art, and table activities (such as puzzles and toys). The young people attend from the age of 16 years, but the majority are in their twenties, and have had little schooling.

1. Ewan

A partially sighted young man joined a group of seven or eight residents attending music sessions. Some showed a little ability to participate actively, others benefitted from the happy atmosphere in the room. Ewan's interest could not be aroused. When given a drum stick he would beat aimlessly for a brief period, apparently unaware of the music being played to him. Now and again Ewan could be persuaded to sing a phrase of his own to a familiar tune (his speech is echolalic). This showed that he had a sense of pitch but, because of the rarity of these occasions, progress could not be made.

Ewan entered and left the music room, making very little impression and gaining little, for several years. Then for several months his health deteriorated. At this time he would sit and pull his jumper over his head, shutting out the world as effectively as possible. When his health began to improve, new songs were introduced to the group, and it became easier to persuade Ewan to sing. His interest in the drum developed when asked to beat a rhythm to the words of a song. When introduced to the guitar, he quickly learned to strum while the leader changed the chords and sang.

Ewan's attitude to coming to sessions has changed noticeably. Now he strides up the hill instead of dragging his feet. Twice a week he can "be someone". He is "Ewan — the person who is good at music". He is able to sing whole songs through — word and note perfect — to a piano accompaniment, strum a guitar, and sing at the same time (with the group leader holding the guitar and changing the chords), and beat a rhythm on chime bars. His repetitive speech has become more relevant, for example:

Leader: "Would you like a drink, Ewan?"
Ewan: "May I have a drink please?"
Leader: "What would you like to drink?"
Ewan: "A drink of orange or lemon please".
Leader: "Do you want to go to the toilet?"
Ewan: "NO!" (if there is a piece of music which he enjoys being played at the end of the session).

Ward staff have been encouraged by his progress, and speak to and sing with him, thus enriching his daily life. His repertoire of songs is increasing. He learns words and melody very quickly and is developing his drumming to a piano accompaniment. Perhaps the most important aspect is that someone with little ability and an extremely limited life-style can make progress in one area, and can be actively and happily engaged in something he obviously enjoys.

2. Thomas

Thomas might as well have displayed a placard saying: "Danger, keep your distance!" If approached he would retreat or hit out. Tension and anxiety were written all over him.

Music sessions at first had little appeal to him, but at least he sat on a chair by a table instead of seeking shelter in corners. The obvious aim was to remove these barriers and to gain his confidence. We began sessions by singing "Hello" to each of the residents present, and shaking hands. At first Thomas would barely allow his fingers to be touched — he hid his face, closed his eyes, and leaned backwards. Session by session and week by week he allowed the contact to grow, until he had sufficient confidence to reach out and shake hands firmly.

Learning to beat the drum became the next step. Thomas would hold a drum stick and tap a drum, so the group leader stood beside him, beat the drum twice, raised her arm high, then beat twice again. Through shy, half-closed eyes, Thomas realised what was happening and, after a while, he began to copy. Later he beat the drum three times, or could alternate as directed.

We wondered whether this could ever develop into his following the rhythmic pattern of a song, or a piano accompaniment. The leader began singing a song and beating its rhythm. Thomas joined in and, after a few weeks, could follow quite well. When the same song was played on the piano in a later session, he not only beat the drum but gave the most accurate performance so far.

Has his progress during music made any difference to his attitude in general and toward other activities? Thomas is less nervous than before, and he does not hit out. There is still plenty of room for improvement, but his ability to mix with other residents and staff in a more relaxed way has improved noticeably. He has begun to join in other activities. Anxiety previously prevented his entering the "free expression" room (sand and water play) despite repeated efforts to coax him in. Now he enters the room, removes his clothing, joins other residents in the shallow pool, and enjoys having water thrown over his body. During movement and music sessions, lessened imaginary fears allow him to link hands with other residents and helpers, and join in with a variety of activities. He recently joined a small group in the recreation hall for a weekly half-hour session of drama and music. Thomas' immediate, happy response to activities is quite remarkable, and his willingness to watch and copy actions demonstrates a great change in his attitude. Anxiety is leaving him, to be replaced by an enjoyment of simple pleasures.

3. Douglas

Douglas is a young man in his twenties who comes from a musical family. It was always obvious that Douglas enjoyed music. His mother had taught him to sing nursery rhymes and carols as a little boy, and had encouraged him to play notes on a key-board. However, he had great anxiety of people and objects around him, hitting anything that touched him. His ability is very limited — not only is he severely mentally handicapped with little speech, but he is also blind. This disability had confined him to a chair all day unless he was led around as, unlike most blind people, he did not attempt to walk unaided.

Douglas began to attend the training unit every morning. At first he displayed his usual anxiety, and his ability in the music room was not remarkable. He could tap on a xylophone given encouragement to do so. Later, as the beat became less hesistant, he seemed to harmonise with any music being played. Attempts to aid him in finding a melody met with a rebuff. About a year after his first attendance at the unit he was sitting in the music room with the xylophone, waiting for other residents to arrive. Suddenly, we heard a melody emerging. When given the first note he played other melodies in following sessions. He learned new tunes quickly. Now he can play melodies on request (not *always* the one asked for), finding the first note himself.

Douglas had always held his limbs stiff, but movement sessions have helped to relax him. Individual exercises have aided his participation in group activities. Since the age of three years he had refused to sit on the floor or the ground, making it necessary to provide a chair for him on family picnics, and reducing his participation in group movement and music activities. By sitting him on a foam-filled block he gradually sank lower until, one day, he accepted the floor. The next step — to persuade him to lie down — was overcome by taking him by surprise on one occasion when he was sitting on the floor. Two staff gently lay him down and talked to him quietly, whilst prostrate, for a few seconds. Subsequently he lay down when requested, and he can now join in all the floor exercises with the other residents.

Douglas' mother provided him with a xylophone for use on the ward, and staff sing with him from time to time. His habit of hitting anything near him has diminished. He will now walk across a room when called, and his enjoyment of life is obvious.

4. Isobella

It is difficult to know the best way to develop a music programme to include handicapped people confined to wheelchairs. Isobella, a dark-haired young woman with a lovely smile, cannot stand. She has limited use of only one hand. She attempts to play notes on a xylophone but her aim is poor. She responds to the singing of her name, but most of all she enjoys holding sleigh bells and shaking them enthusiastically during a song.

She has recently developed an interest in a large drum. She likes to sit where she can see herself in a mirror, then she beats excitedly with the drum stick, accompanied by the piano. As yet she has no sense of the pianist's rhythm change, but varies her own beat and volume slightly. The pianist follows her lead, hoping that she will begin to feel this and respond.

To help Isobella's physical condition a series of exercises to music have been developed. Twice a week her limbs are gently exercised one at a time. At first she started crying as soon as she touched the floor. Now she usually enjoys the exercises. Her legs now extend further than they did when the exercises began. If the exercises could be carried out daily more improvement might be visible.

5. Jason

This young man is also confined to a wheelchair, and is physically more handicapped than Isobella. He has an enlarged head, is blind, and is very physically deformed. He can hear but makes no attempt to communicate. He is fed and changed like a baby.

When in the music room Jason shows a noticeable liking for classical music, swaying his head gently from side to side and smiling. It is a surprise to hear him sing — he is able to sing the melody of several songs (the *Z Cars* theme is his favourite). Sometimes, when these melodies are played and sung to him, tears roll down his face. Are these tears of joy that someone is trying to reach into his enclosed world? We do not know. We can only hope that he feels real pleasure when music is addressed to him.

6. Dorothy

Although her legs cannot be straightened sufficiently for Dorothy to walk she moves around rapidly, crawling on her knees with her body erect. She attended music sessions over a period of about three years. At first she enjoyed the atmosphere of the session and "played" a xylophone, or beat a tambourine. Gradually her interest waned until eventually she just entered the room, sat on a chair, and did nothing.

One day we challenged her to beat a drum twice at the end of each line of the song, *If you're happy and you know it* . . . . She quickly realised what we wanted and repeated it after a few attempts. We moved on to more difficult songs and rhythms which she copied accurately. Her full attention had been gained and a new Dorothy attended music sessions. She began to join in songs (her speech is extremely limited and distorted). She was able to say "where" and "when" at the appropriate time in a song, and even make a good attempt at saying, "What shall we do today?"

Having awoken her latent ability we decided to try teaching her a sign vocabulary*. Her ability to learn signs surprised us. Having learned the first five signs in a couple of weeks (during a group session for five residents, for half an hour, twice a week) she began to learn more signs rapidly. On one

*Makaton Sign Vocabulary

be an aid when bathing, toileting, and dressing him.

Experience with Edward shows the importance of observing the individual to see where strengths and weaknesses lie and the building of a programme based on the results of this observation. It is also important that there is sufficient flexibility in the training programmes, so that residents with similar needs can be grouped together, or so that groups can be balanced to aid programme and individual development.

9. Harry

The residents who attend music or other training sessions are not transformed overnight; in most cases many months of work pass with little result. Harry is particularly difficult. He is extremely excitable and noisy and, although he cannot hold a conversation, he chatters and shouts all day long (a jumble of words and sounds). Understandably his inclusion in a music group causes problems.

Music is meaningful to Harry. When happy he hums a tune to himself and he has been known to hum a complete tune perfectly from beginning to end during a music session. He likes the *Touch-a-Tune organ* and this is used to help to control him during a group session. He is happy to sit by it with the volume turned low so that he can just hear it, but so that it does not disturb others in the room. From that position he will shake bells and tambourines, beat the drum, and participate in action songs to a limited degree. The group programme can then continue, with Harry being involved whenever possible.

10. Joseph

This young man, who looks little more than 12 years old, is over 20. He is mentally handicapped with autistic features.

He is very mobile, pacing up and down the room all day long. The spoken word means little to him. A while ago he wouid not sit on a chair for more than a second. Daily training to sit for short periods during activities (such as passing a ball around a circle) has helped him to sit for longer periods. In music sessions it was necessary at first to sit him on a chair in the corner of the room, with a table in front of him so that he was less able to stand up and pace the room. When still, he has more chance to notice things and to hear what is happening in the room. He has progressed and will now sit with the rest of the group around a large table for up to 20 minutes.

Joseph's response to music is limited, as is his response to everything else. He registers dislike of dischords played on an instrument, and smiles a little when they change to a melodic sound. He sometimes responds to his name being sung by smiling, and he has fleeting eye contact with the singer. He responds to the tempo of music when he walks around the room: his pace varies according to the tempo of the music. As he either chews drum sticks or throws them away it is not yet possible to make use of his feel for tempo on a drum. He is encouraged to join in with music and movement but needs one-to-one attention to participate.

11. Amber

When mentally handicapped adults leave school it can be a difficult time for them, and for those who care for them. The least able people may not be able to attend an adult training centre. What happens to them if the interest and routine of school suddenly stops at school leaving age? They may be at home all day or, in a hospital situation, they may remain on the ward.

Amber became very bored when the younger residents on her ward went out to school. Fortunately for her, the hospital caters for individuals with very little ability in a purpose-built training unit which provides programmes for severely mentally handicapped adults. She now attends the unit five mornings a week. (In other hospitals where such units are not available, activities, training, and recreational pursuits are sometimes organised on the wards.)

Amber is an attractive young woman, who walks with support and is toilet trained. She has frequent epileptic seizures and is also very stubborn. She has more ability than she is prepared to use. During music sessions she is capable of holding and using all the equipment but usually refuses to participate. Her interest lies in singing. She can hum any tune played and loves listening to records and singing along with them. (Her parents take her out in the car and play cassettes to her, her two favourite activities.)

During music sessions Amber hums to live music and is able to sing some of the words. She can count to 10 so she enjoys any counting songs. She is encouraged to use an instrument occasionally, but still flatly refuses. In music and movement sessions she is supported and walks around the room, usually enjoying all the exercises; occasionally refusing to join in and clinging like a limpet to her chair. To avoid activities she sometimes simulates a fit.

During music a genuine fit can be triggered by a continuous note being played (for example, the needle sticking on a record, or a resident holding on to one note on the *Touch-a-Tune*). Amber is likely to have a fit if approached from behind and touched, or if her chair is pushed suddenly by another resident.

This young woman's life is considerably enriched by music and the daily change of environment. If suitable activities are not provided for them, hospital residents sometimes develop bad behaviour to occupy themselves or to attract the attention of the staff. It is far easier to prevent this happening than to stop it once it is established.

Note. Since this was written Amber has begun to hold and shake bells, and beat a drum.

12. David

This young man has a behaviour problem. Although over 20 years of age he is small, has poor balance, and needs support to walk. He has no recognisable speech but wants to communicate. His sight is poor and his fingers cannot work independently.

Comparing him with others who attend music he seems quite bright. He is able to understand what is said and share a joke, but his bad behaviour ruins his enjoyment of life and his chances of improvement. During outbursts he will kick, throw anything within reach, and purposely injure himself. This pattern has built up over the years, possibly because of a lack of means to communicate. Now he is learning a sign vocabulary*, but his bad behaviour is difficult to eradicate as it is so well established.

David especially enjoys music and likes to sit on a chair rocking to its beat. If this is denied for any reason it can cause an outburst of temper, but he may begin to misbehave at any time. It is necessary to train him to be part of a group and for him to realise that he cannot have attention all the time, or what he wants at the moment he wants it. He

*Makaton Sign Vocabulary

comes to music sessions with eight other residents. Activities consist of a *Good morning* song, when everyone shakes hands with his neighbour, a *name* song (for example, "Where is Tony Brooks? . . . Here I am . . ."), movement of different parts of the body to music while sitting on chairs, individual "singing" or miming of a song, and listening to music.

David is learning to co-operate and anticipates the next activity. He knows that if he misbehaves he will be temporarily withdrawn from the music session. If he co-operates well all morning during several different sessions (such as music, sign language, "free expression", and music and movement) he is rewarded with a cup of tea and a biscuit. A careful plan for his treatment has been drawn up through discussion with his doctor and all the staff responsible for his care in order to ensure a consistent approach in all areas (i.e. ward, training unit, recreation hall) throughout the day.

13. Cyril

This young man began to attend music sessions several years ago. We were told that he could pick out melodies on a piano using one or two fingers. He was very withdrawn, apprehensive of other residents, and did not speak (although he used to have some speech as a small child). He could not be motivated and just sat in a chair all day, only moving when told to sit at the table or go to the toilet. He could not be classified as profoundly mentally handicapped, yet his added problems caused him to operate at a level well below his ability. Occasionally he would have outbursts of temper and throw his shoes, push over chairs, and scream and roll on the floor.

In the group music session he joined Cyril first learned to play the xylophone in time to an accompaniment. This took some weeks to establish. Then he led the group, with others beating a drum, and shaking bells or tambourines. At the end of each music session he received a five minute lesson to teach him to use all his fingers on the piano. He learned scales and arpeggios quite easily.

Gradually Cyril's confidence grew and he began to tolerate other residents, even when they bumped into him or shouted near him. He joined in with music and movement and attended sign language sessions.* He learned signs rapidly and could soon sign whole sentences and answer questions with the words in the correct order. We could then see how much ability Cyril had locked within himself, but still he did not want to communicate and used signing only during signing sessions.

Eventually Cyril improved sufficiently to be able to attend the industrial training unit. From there he attends movement and music sessions once a week in the recreation hall. With an occasional prompt he will run, leap, crawl, jump, and follow instructions and activities. Whilst in the hall he plays the piano at the beginning and end of the session, using the arpeggios he has learned to make chords and to harmonise. For Cyril, music has a very special place in his development and it can really be a key to unlock his ability.

**Paget Gorman Sign System* (begun before the advent of *Makaton*)

14. Geoffrey

We are very interested in the reactions produced by various types of music. Most mentally handicapped people respond at once to "pop" music, with which they are most familiar. From the point of view of training this is of little value (although it can occasionally be used to stimulate a resident to hold a drum stick and begin to beat on a drum because of the very strong beat of such music). As the majority of residents rock to and fro to this music and show pleasure, inexperienced staff may be tempted to play "pop" records and allow everyone to make a loud noise on any instruments available. This has no value and tends to dull sensitivity to musical sounds. Some staff forget that not all residents enjoy "pop" music. To some it may be upsetting, and Geoffrey is one of these.

We played various types of music for Geoffrey, including country and western, "pop", classical orchestral, and organ music. The rest of the group enjoyed the music with the strong beat. Geoffrey bit his hand, hit his head with his hand, and shouted. When we played the organ music his attitude changed at once. He stood up and, as if in a trance, walked around the room gazing upwards. We played him this music on a number of occasions and each time it had the same effect on him.

In the light of this it seems important to consider the likes and dislikes of residents. When music is played as a background, in a ward, for example, staff should introduce variety and not allow constant "pop" music to bombard the residents from dawn to bedtime.

15. Ronald

Ronald, who attended music sessions some years ago, showed no reaction to music at all. He is a person locked within his own small world with no apparent interest in his environment. Various efforts have been made to bring awareness to him (for example, by a feeding programme, toilet training, and eye contact) but nothing has succeeded. The only sounds he makes are whistles and chirps.

One day he was in the music room with a small group of residents and several staff had gathered to try the instruments for themselves. We played xylophones in unison to a keyboard accompaniment of the tune, *When the Saints go marching in.* When a tape-recording of this was played back we heard — to our amazement — Ronald's voice, at first making his usual sounds and then gradually moving to the pitch of the music and ending up following it. It seemed as if the melody drew him like a magnet until he was one with the music. The incident taught us never to despair over any resident. Somewhere, there is a point of contact with even the most remote individual.

"Angela, lift your arms . . . "

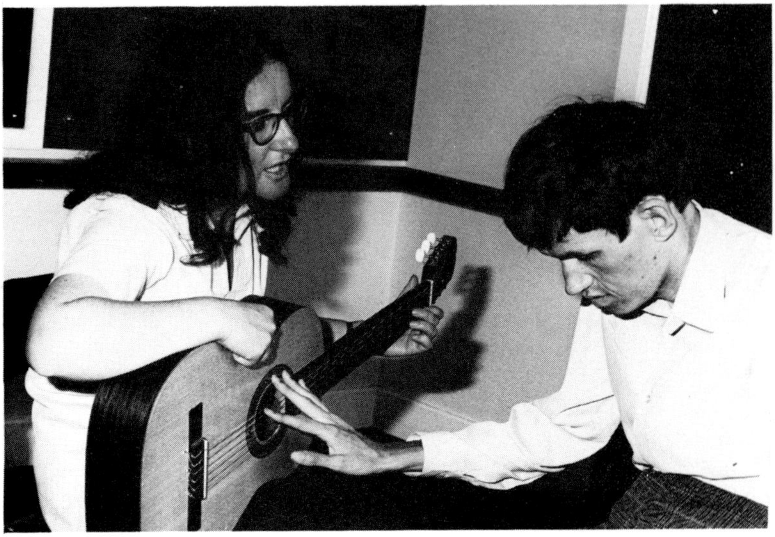

When introduced to a guitar Ewan quickly learned to strum

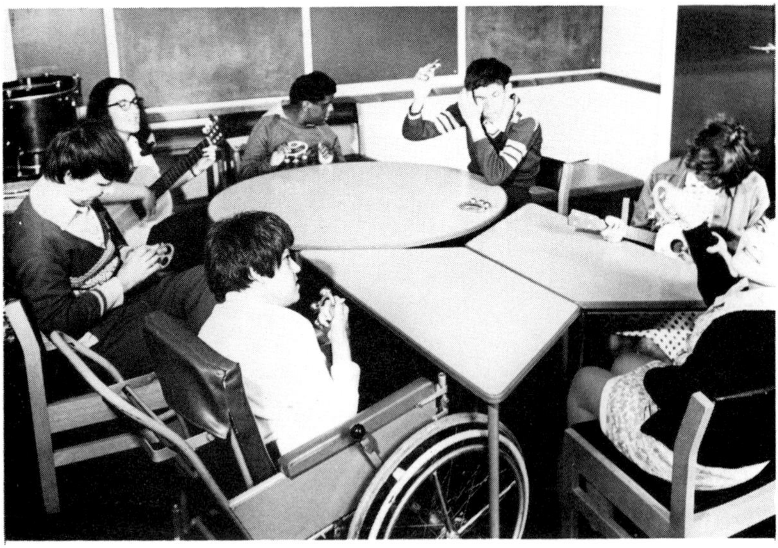

"Shake, shake, shake the bells . . . "

"Hold on tight — and pull!"

Douglas, blind and mentally handicapped, can play melodies and enjoys music very much

Cyril shows real musical ability

Instruments useful for music sessions

Sleigh bells
Wrist bells
Stick bells
Cow bells
Triangles
Maracas
Guitars
Autoharp
Swanee whistles
Duck calls
Bird whistles
Recorders
Melodicas
Tambours
Hard and soft beaters
Chime bars (full set or octave)
Xylophones
Metallaphones
Glockenspiels
Tambourines
Bass drum
Snare drum on stand
Bongo drums
Cymbal and stand
Small cymbal
Piano or chord organ
Touch-a-Tune organ
Tape recorder
Record deck
Drum sticks

The instruments listed can be obtained from most music shops or ordered from school supply catalogues.

Music for listening

Pomp and Circumstance (Land of Hope and Glory)	Elgar
William Tell Overture	Rossini
Slavonic Dances	Dvorjak
Violin Concerto	Bach
Planet Suite	Holst
Symphony No. 9	Beethoven
Clair de Lune	Debussy
Gymnopedies	Satie
Carnival of the Animals	Saint-Saens
Folk music (from various countries)	examples: Swiss yodelling songs, Rumanian pipe music, Scottish bagpipes or folk band music, African tribal songs
Peals of church bells	
The Entertainer	Scot Joplin
Selection from *101 Strings*	Mantovani
Selection from *Big Band Music*	Glen Miller

This brief list gives examples of music suitable for listening to, from the wide range of types of music that may be enjoyed by handicapped people. Short passages can be selected for use in the time available for music sessions.

Song books and reading list

Alvin, J. *Music for the handicapped child* (2nd edn.). London: Oxford University Press, 1976.

Alvin, J. *Music therapy for the autistic child.* London: Oxford University Press, 1978.

Appleby, W., Fowler, F. *Sing together!* London: Oxford University Press, 1967.

Bailey, P. *They can make music.* London: Oxford University Press, 1973.

Baxter, K. *A framework for music making.* 1976. Available from the author: 6 Esher Grove, Mapperley Park, Nottingham, NG3 5DR.

Baxter, K. *Play the Chromaharp.* 1981. Available from the author — see above.

Baxter, K., Thompson, D. *Pompaleerie Jig.* Leeds: E. J. Arnold. (Date not stated.)

Beresford-Peirse, S., du Feu, J., Worthington, J., Nordoff, P. *The Goldie Leigh Song Book.* London: Goldie Leigh Hospital. (Date not stated.)

Birkenshaw, L. *Music for fun, music for learning.* Eastbourne: Holt-Saunders, 1977.

Brocklehurst, B. (Ed.). *Pentatonic Song Book(s)*. London: Schott, Book 1, 1968, Book 2, 1976.

Chatterley, A. *70 Simple Songs with Ostinati.* Sevenoaks: Novello, 1975.

Clarke, C., Chadwick, D. *Clinically adapted instruments for the multiply handicapped: a resource book.* Mass: Modulations, 1979.

Colson, J. *Getting into rhythm.* Harrogate: Yorkshire Regional Health Authority, 1974.

Hunt, A. *Listen — let's make music.* London: Bedford Square Press, 1976 (out of print).

Kennard, D., Gilbertson, M. *Music to help disabled children to move.* Ilkley: Association of Paediatric Chartered Physiotherapists, 1977.

Kennard, D. *Report on Access to Music for the Handicapped School Child and School Leaver,* (2nd Edn.). London: Disabled Living Foundation, 1979.

Kennard, D. *Paper M.P.1.* (This regularly revised list of music books is available from: Disabled Living Foundation (see addresses).

Mendoza, A. *Sociable Songs No. 1: Piano and melody.* London: Oxford University Press, 1970.

Mendoza, A. *Tops and Tails*. London: Oxford University Press, 1968.

Mendoza, A. *More Tops and Tails*. London: Oxford University Press, 1971.

Mendoza, A. *Tops and Tails Again*. London: Oxford University Press, 1976.

Millar, N. *Simple home-made instruments*. Available from the author: 46, Newlands Road, Billericay, Essex.

Moule, S., Williams, L., Holland, J. *Educational rhythmics in practice*. Kidderminster: BIMH, 1979.

Nordoff, P., Robbins, C. *Creative Music Therapy — individualised treatment for the handicapped child* (with tape). New York: John Day, 1978.

Nordoff, P., Robbins, C. *Fun for four drums*. USA: Theodore Presser, 1968.

Nordoff, P., Robbins, C. *Songs for children with resonator bells and piano*. USA: Theodore Presser, 1962.

Nordoff, P., Robbins, C. *The first book of children's play songs*. USA: Theodore Presser, 1962.

Nordoff, P., Robbins, C. *Therapy in music for handicapped children*. London: Gallancz, 1971.

Nordoff, P., Robbins, C. *The second book of children's play songs*. *Pennsylvania*: Bryn Mawr, 1968.

Roberts, R. *Musical Instruments Made to be Played*. Leicester, Dryad, 1965.

Orff, G. *The Orff Music Therapy*. 1980. Available from: Schott, 48 Great Marlborough Street, London.

Upton, G. (Ed.). *Physical and creative activities for the mentally handicapped*. Cambridge University Press, 1979.

Ward, D. *Sing a rainbow*. London: Oxford University Press, 1980.

Ward, D. *Sound approaches for slow learners.* London: Bedford Square Press, 1975.

Warren, M., Spinks, D. *Songs of speech* (book and tape). Available from: Taskmaster, Morris Road, Clarendon Park, Leicester.

Wethered, A. G. *Drama and Movement in Therapy*. Plymouth: Macdonald and Evans, 1973 (out of print).

APPENDIX 4

Addresses

Association of Professional Music Therapists. Contact: Helen Odell, 146 Gilbert Road, Cambridge. Tel: 0223 69717.

Baxter, Kate (Miss), LRAM, 6 Esher Grove, Mapperley Park, Nottingham, NG3 5DR. Tel: 0602 609528. Teacher and Lecturer on music for the handicapped.

Bristol Polytechnic, Redland Hill, Bristol, BS6 6UZ. Tel: 0272 7412. Contact: Mrs. Veronica Sherborne (Room 12, Malvern House), for film and book list on movement for the mentally handicapped.

British Institute of Mental Handicap, Wolverhampton Road, Kidderminster, Worcs., DY10 3PP. Tel: 0562 850251. Quarterly Journal *Mental Handicap*. BIMH Information and Resource Centre. Department of Educational Rhythmics run by Mrs. Shirley Moule.

British Society for Music Therapy, 48, Lanchester Road, London, N6 4TA. Tel: 01-883 1331. Anyone using music for the handicapped and in harmony with their ideas may join. Publish 'Journal of Music Therapy'.

Castle Priory College, Thames Street, Wallingford, Oxfordshire, OX10 0HE. Tel: 0491 37551. Courses on music for the handicapped.

Council for Music in Hospitals, 340, Lower Road, Little Bookham, Surrey, KT23 4EF. Tel: 0372 58264 (office hours). Contact: Sylvia Lindsay. Professional artists give concerts to suit patients in hospitals of all kinds.

Dartington College of Arts, Totnes, Devon, T29 6EJ. Tel: 0803 862224. Three month course (January to March) on Music for Slow Learners. Contact: Mr. David Ward (Music Dept.).

Disabled Living Foundation, 346, Kensington High Street, London, W14 8NS. Tel: 01-602 2491. Miss D. Kennard, Music Advisor for the handicapped.

Early Learning Centre — see telephone book for local centre. Supply strong bells, beaters etc.

Guildhall School of Music and Drama. Tel: 01-883 1331. One year (post grad.) course in Music Therapy. Contact: Miss Juliette Alvin, FGSM, MT. 48, Lanchester Road, London, N6 4TA.

Hestair Hope Ltd., St. Philip's Drive, Royston, Oldham, OL2 6AG. Tel: 061-633 3938. Supply foam shapes, musical instruments, and other strongly constructed equipment.

ILEA Adult Education Training Unit, Room 45, The City Lit., Stukeley Street, Drury Lane, London, WC2B 5LJ. Tel: 01-242 9872. Evening courses on music for the handicapped. Music Swapshop to exchange ideas on music for the handicapped. Contact: Mrs. Janet Wyatt.

MIND, National Association for Mental Health, 22, Harley Street, London, W1N 2ED. Tel: 01-637 0741. Course: Creative Activities for the handicapped.

Natural Dance Society, Playspace, Peto Place, London, NW1 4DT. Three month, evening, weekend, or holiday courses on movement and music which can be related to the handicapped.

Nordoff-Robbins Music Therapy Centre, 3, Leighton Place, London, NW5 2QL. Tel: 01-267 6296. Course: Miss S. Beresford-Peirse runs post-graduate course in co-operation with the City University.

Roehampton Institute of Higher Education, Southlands College, Wimbledon Parkside, London, SW19 5NN. Tel: 01-946 2234. Course: Miss Elaine Streeter runs a full time diploma course.

Royal Society for Mentally Handicapped Children and Adults, 117, Golden Lane, London, EC1Y 0RT. Tel: 01-253 9433. Occasional workshops for those working with the handicapped.

SHAPE, 9 Fitzroy Square, London W1P 6AE. Tel: 01-388 9622 or 9744. Information sheet available, movement and dance. Contact: Miss Seona Reid.

Telemachus Ltd., P.O. Box 86, Aylesbury, Bucks. Tel: 0296 623670. Supplies: 'Touch-a-Tune' Instrument.

The Tibble Trust, 36, Belsize Court, Wedderburn Road, London, NW3 5QJ. Mr. J. K. Owens. Trust arranges three-day courses for groups of hospitals/schools to train staff to use music with the handicapped.

NOTES

NOTES

NOTES

About the author

Music came naturally to Miriam Wood as she was born into a musical family in Wales. She developed an interest in handicapped people early in life through friendship with a neighbour's daughter who has Down's syndrome. As a child she studied piano, singing, and violin. Later at Newbold College, Bracknell she studied general musicianship for three years. Recently she gained a City and Guilds Certificate for Teaching of the Handicapped in Further Education from Bracknell College of Further Education.

The value of music to mentally handicapped people became apparent to her whilst working at a National Children's Home where there were children with various handicaps. She put her ideas into practice when she moved on to work with mentally handicapped adults.

In 1978 the Berkshire Area Health Authority gave her a grant to investigate the use of music with profoundly mentally handicapped adults. She lectures on the subject of music for the mentally handicapped to teachers, nurses, and students, has prepared audiovisual material for a medical library, and has had articles published. She continues to use music daily in her work with mentally handicapped people.

Published and distributed by: British Institute of Mental Handicap

Price: £5.25

ISBN 0 906054 47 8